W9-APL-745

A Running Press® Miniature Edition™
Copyright © 2001 by Warthog Productions
All rights reserved under the Pan-American and International
Copyright Conventions
Printed in China

Library of Congress Cataloging-in-Publication Number 2001117169

ISBN 0-7624-1079-5

This book may be ordered by mail from the publisher. Please include
$1.00 for postage and handling.
But try your bookstore first!

Running Press Book Publishers
125 South Twenty-second Street
Philadelphia, Pennsylvania 19103-4399

Visit us on the web!
www.runningpress.com

A few years ago, we wanted to bring some peace to family mealtimes, and teach our kids—and ourselves—gratitude. So we collected simple graces from many different cultures, put them in a box on the kitchen table, and took turns selecting a new one to read aloud each night. A tradition was born: a box of blessings to "grace" the table and warm the heart. We hope these words of thanks help you, as they have helped us. appreciate the gifts of each new day: food, family, laughter, love, and life itself.

Laurada Byers and Joseph Torsella

i thank You God for most this
amazing day: for the leaping
greenly spirits of trees and a blue
true dream of sky; and for
    everything
which is natural which is
infinite which is yes
how should tasting touching
    hearing seeing
breathing any-lifted from the
no of all nothing-human merely
being doubt unimaginable You?

E. E. Cummings, (c) 1950

Sweet is the work,
my God, my King,

To praise thy name,
give thanks and sing.

Methodist Hymn,
19th Century

May we be a channel of blessings
for all that we meet.

Edgar Cayce, Clairvoyant,
1877–1945

Not for the mighty world,
O Lord, tonight,

Nations and kingdoms in their
fearful might,

Let me be glad the kettle gently sings,

Let me be glad for little things.

Edna Jaques,
1891–1978

Give us thankful hearts . . .
Let us seize the day and the opportunity
and strive for that Greatness of spirit
that measures life not by its
    disappointments
But by its possibilities, and let us
    ever remember
that true gratitude and appreciation
    shows itself
neither in independence not satisfaction
but passes the gift joyfully on in larger
    and better form.

W.E.B. DuBois

When I'm worried and
I can't sleep,

I count my blessings instead of sheep.

And I fall asleep counting
my blessings.

When my bankroll is
getting small,

I think of when I had none at all.

And I fall asleep counting
my blessings.

Irving Berlin, (c) 1952

Lord, behold our family here assembled.
We thank you for this place
in which we dwell,
For the love that unites us,
For the peace accorded us this day.
For the hope with which
we expect tomorrow;
For the health, the work, the food
And the bright skies
that make our lives delightful.
Amen.

Robert Louis Stevenson, 1850–1894

Give me good digestion, Lord,

And also something
to digest.

Give me a healthy body, Lord,

and sense to keep it
at its best.

Give me a healthy mind,
good Lord,

To keep the good and pure in sight,

Which, seeing sin, is not appalled,

But finds a way to set it right.

Give me a sense of humor, Lord,

Give me the grace to see a joke,

To get some happiness
from life

And pass it on to other folk.

Thomas H. B. Webb, 1898–1917
England

We thank Thee for all our daily bread,
We thank Thee for all our friends so true,
For fields and flow'rs and mountains high.
The endless space of the sky so blue.

We thank Thee for all the winding roads,
We thank Thee for all the stars so bright,
For desert sands and forests green.
The campfires glow in the lovely night.

Traveler's Grace
(an excerpt from Girl Scouts'
Pocket Songbook)

Thou that hast given
so much to me,

Give one thing more,
a grateful heart.

Not thankful when it
pleaseth me,

As if thy blessings
had spare days;

But such a heart, whose pulse
may be thy praise.

George Herbert,
1593–1633

An easy thing, O Power Divine,

To thank Thee for these gifts of Thine,

For summer's sunshine,
winter's snow,

For hearts that kindle,
thoughts that glow;

But when shall I attain to this

To thank Thee for the things
I miss?

*Thomas Wentworth Higginson,
19th Century*

No longer forward nor behind
I look for hope or fear;
But, grateful, take the good I find,
The best of now and here.

John Greenleaf Whittier,
1807–1893

Be present at our table, Lord

Be here and everywhere adored

Thy creatures bless and grant that we

May feast in paradise with Thee.

John Cennick, 1718–1755

O Thou who clothes the lilies,

Who feeds the birds of the sky,

Who leads the lambs to pasture,

And the deer to the waterside,

Who multiplies loaves and fishes,

And changed the water to wine,

Do Thou come to our table as giver

And as our guest to dine.

Anonymous

The Baby's Grace

Praise to God who giveth meat

Convenient unto all to want:

Praise for tea and buttered toast,

Father, Son and Holy Ghost.

R. L. Gales (England)

For water-ices, cheap but good,
That find us in a thirsty mood;
For ices made of milk or cream
That slip down smoothly as a dream;
For cornets, sandwiches and pies
That make the gastric juices rise;
For ices brought in little shops
Or at the kerb from him who stops;
For chanting of the sweet refrain:
"Vanilla, strawberry or plain?"
We thank Thee, Lord, who sendst with heat
This cool deliciousness to eat.

The Ice Cream Blessing,
Allan M. Laing England

Back of the loaf is
the snowy flour,

And back of the flour
the mill,

And back of the mill is
the wheat, and the shower,

And the sun,
and the Father's will.

M. D. Babcock, 1858–1901
England

May all who share
These gifts today
Be blessed by Thee,
We humbly pray.

Be the meal
Of beans or peas, God be thanked
For those and these.

Have we flesh

Or have we fish,

All are fragments

From his dish.

Robert Herrick, 1591–1674
England

To God who gives our daily bread
A thankful song we raise,
And pray that he who sends us food
May fill our hearts with praise.

Thomas Tallis, 1505–1585

Give us, O Lord, thankful
hearts which never forget
Your goodness to us.
Give us, O Lord, grateful
hearts, which do not waste
time complaining.

Saint Thomas Aquinas,
1225–1274

It is a comely fashion to be glad;

Joy is the grace we say to god.

Socrates, 470 B.C.–399 B.C.
Greece

Praised be my Lord
for our mother me earth,

that which doth sustain us
and keep us, and

bringeth forth diverse fruit,
and flowers of many

colours, and grass.

Saint Francis of Assisi,
1182–1228

A single grateful
thought raised to heaven is the
most perfect prayer.

Gotthold Ephraim Lessing, 1729–1781
German

Now thank we all our God

With heart and hands and voices,

Who wondrous things hath done,

In whom this world rejoices;

Who, from our mothers' arms,

Hath blessed us on our way

With countless gifts of love,

And still is ours today.

Martin Rinkart, 1636

We thank thee, Lord, for happy hearts,

For rain and sunny weather;

We thank thee, Lord, for this our food,

And that we are together.

Traditional Mennonite Blessing

Bless these Thy gifts,
most gracious God,

From whom all goodness springs;

Make clean our hearts
and feed our souls

With good and joyful things.

Traditional Christian grace

Lord Jesus, be our holy guest,

Our morning Joy, our evening rest,

And with our daily bread impart

Your love and peace to every heart.

Traditional Christian Grace

O giver of each perfect gift!
This day our daily bread supply:
While from the Spirit's tranquil depths
We drink unfailing draughts of joy.

Lyra Catholica

Joining hands:
Everyone at the table
joins hands for a
silent moment.

Quaker grace

Go thy way,
eat thy bread with joy,
and drink thy wine
with a merry heart.

Ecclesiastes 9:7

May the Lord bless
Us with Sabbath joy.
May the lord bless us
with Sabbath Holiness.
May the Lord bless us
with Sabbath peace.

Traditional Jewish Sabbath Blessing

Scones and pancakes roun' the table,

Eat as much as ye are able,

Eat! Leave Nothing!

Hallelujah! Amen.

Scottish Traditional

Bless to me, O God,

Each thing mine eye sees;

Bless to me, O God,

Each sound mine ear hears;

Bless to me, O God,

Each odour that goes to my nostrils;

Bless to me, O God,

Each taste that goes to my lips. . . .

Ancient Celtic Prayer

Let us in peace eat the food
that God has provided for us.
Praise be to God for all
his gifts. Amen

Ancient Armenian Grace

May the blessing of five
loaves and two fishes
which God divided amongst
Five thousand men be ours,
And may the King Who made
division put luck in our
food and in our portion. Amen.

Irish Blessing

Some hae meat, and canna eat,

And some wad eat that want it;

But we hae meat, an' we can eat,

And sae the Lord be thankit.

Robert Burns, 1759–1796
Scotland

Give us Lord, a bit o'sun,

A bit o'work and a bit o'fun;

Give us all in the struggle and sputter

Our daily bread and a bit o'butter.

On the wall of an old inn
Lancaster, England

Lord most giving and resourceful, I implore you: make it your will that this people enjoy the goods and riches you naturally give, that naturally issue from you, that are pleasing and savory, that delight and comfort, though lasting but briefly, passing away as if in a dream.

Aztec, Mexico

Book of Blessings

O my Father, Great Elder,

I have no words to thank you,

But with your deep wisdom

I am sure that you can see

How I value your glorious gifts.

O Great Elder,

Ruler of all things earthly and heavenly,

I am your warrior,

Ready to act in accordance
with your will.

Kikuyu Blessing
Kenya

O you who feed the little bird,

bless our food, O Lord.

Traditional Norwegian

God of my needfulness,

grant me something to eat,

give me milk,

give me sons,

give me herds,

give me meat,

O my Father.

Morning Invocation, African

Thank you, kind Father,
for giving us food to make our bodies
grow stronger. Dear God, teach us
to share with others what we
ourselves have. Amen.

Chinese Child's Prayer

May it be pleasing to Allah!

Traditional Islamic Blessing

O God our Lord,
send a table down to
us from heaven above.
Make the day of
its coming like a
festival for us,
for Thou art the best
provider.

The Koran

Innumerable labors
have brought us this food.
We should know how it comes to us.
As we receive this offering
we should consider whether our
practice and virtue deserve it.

Soto Buddhist blessing

This ritual is One
The food is One
We who offer the food are One
The fire of hunger is also One
All action is One
We who understand this are One.

Hindu blessing

He is God!

behold us, O Lord, gathered at this
board,

thankful for Thy bounty,

our gaze turned to thy kingdom.

Verily, Thou art the generous, and verily,

Thou art the Beneficent, the Merciful.

Abdu'l-Baha, Iran

This we know.
The earth does not belong to us,
   we belong to the earth.
   This we know.
All things are connected
like the blood which unites one family.
All things are connected.

Whatever befalls the earth
Befalls the sons and daughters
   of the earth.

We did not weave the web of life,
We are merely a strand in it.
Whatever we do to the web,
we do to ourselves . . .

Chief Seattle, 1786–1866
Written by Ted Perry,
inspired by a speech by Chief Seattle

Book of Blessings

Dear God, bless those who
bear the hardship of famine
and those who share their
plenty with others.
Wrap Thy love around those
who come to us in trust
and take care of those who
wander far from us in anger.
Amen.

Early Hawaiian food prayer

O Lord, the meal is steaming before us and it smells good. The water is clear and fresh. We are happy and satisfied. But now we must think of our sisters and brothers all over the world who have nothing to eat and only a little to drink. Please, please give all of them your food and your drink. That is most important. But give them also what they need every day to go through this life.

Amen.

Prayers by Young Africans

Book of Blessings

The lands around my dwelling

Are more beautiful

From the day

When it is given to me to see

Faces I have never seen before.

All is more beautiful,

All is more beautiful,

And life is thankfulness.

These guests of mine

Make my house grand.

Eskimo

For Food,
For Raiment,
For Life,
For Opportunity,
For Friendship
And Fellowship,
We thank Thee, O Lord.
Amen.

Philmont Scout Ranch Grace

Acknowledgments and Permissions

Grateful acknowledgement is made to the authors and publishers for use of the following material. Every effort has been made to assign proper credits for selections. If any have been omitted where due, we will gladly include them in subsequent editions.

Boy Scouts of America, "Philmont Scout Ranch Grace," used by permission of the Boy Scouts of America.

Richard of Chichester, "Prayer For The New Year," Prayer Poems, An Anthology compiled and arranged by O.V. & Helen Armstrong, (Nashville: Abingdon Press).

R. L. Gales, "The Baby's Grace," Prayers and Graces, collected by Allen Laing, (London: Victor Gollancz Ltd, 1944) p. 33.

Dag Hammerskjold, trans., Auden/Sjoberg, Markings, Translation Copyright (c) 1964 by Alfred A. Knopf, Inc. and Faber & Faber Ltd. Reprinted by permission of Alfred A. Knopf, a Division of Random House, Inc. (Random House)

Thomas Wentworth Higginson, "The Things I Miss," Prayer Poems, An Anthology compiled and arranged by O.V. & Helen Armstrong, (Nashville: Abingdon Press), p. 25.

Grenville Kleiser, "My Daily Prayer." Prayer Poems, An Anthology compiled and arranged by O.V. & Helen Armstrong, (Nashville: Abingdon Press).

A.M.L., "A Grace for Ice–Cream," Allen Laing, "The Ice Cream Blessing" and "The Baby's Grace," Prayers and Graces, p. 34.

Robert Louis Stevenson, "Lord, behold our family here assembled," Good Graces, Table Prayers, collected by Julie Jensen McDonald, (Iowa: Penfield Press, 1986) p. 16.

Evelyn Stobie, "Traveler's Grace," from Girl Scout Pocket Songbook, copyright (c) 1956, Girl Scouts of the USA., p. 21.

W.E.B. DuBois, "Give us thankful hearts," Prayers for Dark People, edited by Herbert Aptheker, (Amherst: University of Massachusetts Press, 1980), p.12.

Prayers by Young Africans, "The Meal Is Steaming," I Lie on My Mat and Pray, edited by Fritz Pawelzik, translated from the German by Robbins Strong. (New York: Friendship Press, 1964), p. 102.

The lines from "i thank You God for this amaz-

Most of the text
and photographs in this Running Press®
Miniature Edition™ is excerpted
from *Bless This Home*, a kit also published
by Running Press.

This book has been bound
using handcraft methods and Smyth-sewn
to ensure durability.

The text was edited by Molly Jay

The text was set in Adobe Caslon, Coronet,
Papyrus, and Type Embellishments